Essential COO_____S

COMPREHENSIVE, STEP BY S_____ ___OKING

Sweet
Treats

BUDGET
BOOKS

Food Editor: Neil Hargreaves
Cover Design: Budget Books
Prepress: Graphic Print Group

Essential Cooking Series: Sweet Treats
First published in 2008 by Budget Books Pty Ltd
45–55 Fairchild Street
Heatherton, Victoria, 3202, Australia

10 9 8 7 6 5
13 12 11 10 09

Disclaimer: The nutritional information listed under each recipe does not
include the nutrient content of garnishes or any accompaniments not listed
in specific quantitites in the ingredient list. The nutritional information for
each recipe is an estimate only, and may vary depending on the brand of
ingredients used, and due to natural biological variations in the composition
of natural foods such as meat, fish, fruit and vegetables. The nutritional
information was calculated by using Foodworks dietary analysis software
(Version 3, Xyris Software Pty Ltd, Highgate Hill, Queensland, Australia) based
on the Australian food composition tables and food manufacturers' data.
Where not specified, ingredients are always analysed as average or medium,
not small or large.

ISBN: 978 1 7418 1464 4

Printed and bound in China

Contents

introduction   4–7

fruit and nut slices   8–16

chocolate slices   17–31

fruit and nut biscuits   32–43

chocolate biscuits   44–57

glossary   58–59

conversions   60–61

index   62–63

An introduction to sweet treats

Nothing smells more like home cooking than a tray full of hot biscuits or slices ready to be cut into squares or fingers. Whether it's kids' lunches, after-school goodies or treats for all the family on the weekend, there is always a place for home-baked slices and biscuits. Each recipe in this book gives you clear instructions on how to prepare the treats you have chosen to cook. As with all baking, there are a few rules that should be adhered to and a few traps that you don't want to fall into, but generally biscuits and slices are the most trouble-free things to bake!

In general, you should always measure your ingredients accurately when baking, and substitute ingredients with others that are close in weight and moisture if you do vary a recipe. A good tip for baking slices is to use a sheet of baking paper to line the baking tray, making the slice less likely to stick and easier to move after cutting up.

Biscuits should be laid out on trays with enough room for them to spread while they bake and set, but not so far apart so that you

can only bake a few at a time. Each biscuit recipe responds a little differently in this way, so look at the finished biscuits you bake for distances between them: when you bake them again you can adjust the distances to get the maximum biscuits per tray.

Always allow your treats to fully cool down before putting them away, and always store them in an airtight container: this way biscuits and slices will last for a couple of weeks.

To decorate some of the slices in this book you'll need to make a piping bag to pipe warm chocolate. This technique can be used on any of the slices that have chocolate in them or have flavours that are complementary to chocolate.

You can also cut out designs in greaseproof paper and use them as stencils to dust either cocoa or icing sugar over them! Use your imagination and cut out stars and hearts, or coat slices with a layer of icing and 100s and 1000s; it's up to you how far you take the decorating.

MAKING A PAPER PIPING BAG

1 Cut a 25 cm square of greaseproof paper. Cut the square in half diagonally to form two triangles.

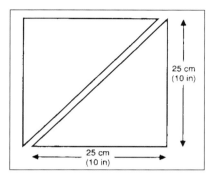

2 To make the piping bag, place the paper triangles on top of each other and mark the three corners A, B and C.

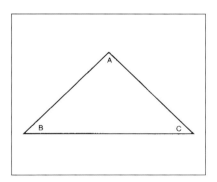

3 Fold corner B around and inside corner A.

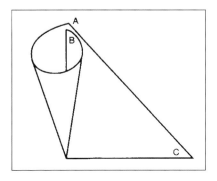

4 Bring corner C around the outside of the bag until it fits exactly behind corner A. At this stage all three corners should be together and the point closed.

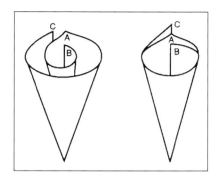

5 Fold corner A over two or three times to hold the bag together. Snip the point off the bag and drop into an icing nozzle. The piping bag can also be used without a nozzle for writing and outlines, in which case only the very tip of the point should be snipped off.

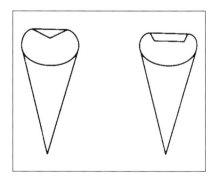

PIPED CHOCOLATE DECORATIONS

You can use piped chocolate decorations to decorate cakes, pastries and desserts, and they are quick and easy to make. Trace a simple design onto a sheet of paper. Tape a sheet of greaseproof paper to your work surface and slide the drawings under the paper. Place melted chocolate into a paper or material piping bag (see instructions on page 5) and, following the tracings, pipe thin lines. Allow to set at room temperature and then carefully remove using a metal spatula. If you're not going to use the decorations immediately, store them in an airtight container in a cool place.

FILLING A PIPING BAG

Spoon chocolate or icing into the bag until half-full. Fold about 1 cm of the bag over, then fold over again. Fold the tips towards the centre, folding the top in half and pressing your thumb on the join to force the chocolate or icing out.

USING A PIPING BAG

Grip the piping bag near the top, with the folded or twisted end held between the thumb and fingers. Guide the bag with your free hand. Right-handed people should decorate from left to right, while left-handers need to decorate from right to left, except when piping writing.

The appearance of your piping will be directly affected by how much you squeeze or relax your grip on the piping bag: that is, the pressure you apply and the steadiness of that pressure. The pressure should be so consistent that you can move the bag in a free and easy glide with just the right amount of chocolate or icing flowing from the nozzle. A little practice will soon have you feeling confident.

Fruit medley slice

INGREDIENTS

base
100 g butter
125 g self-raising flour
155 g brown sugar
90 g desiccated coconut
filling
250 g dried fruit medley
4 tablespoons orange juice
155 g brown sugar
6 tablespoons butter, melted
60 g pecans, chopped
45 g desiccated coconut
topping
200 g white chocolate, melted
makes 12

PREPARATION TIME
10 minutes

COOKING TIME
30 minutes

1 Preheat the oven to 180°C. Combine the butter, flour, brown sugar and coconut. Mix well. Press mixture into a greased 30 x 20 cm baking tin. Bake for 15 minutes.

2 Meanwhile, soak the fruit medley in the orange juice for 10 minutes. Combine with brown sugar, melted butter, pecans and coconut. Mix well.

3 Remove the baking tin from the oven and pour the filling over the base. Then return to the oven and cook for a further 15 minutes. Cool in the tin.

4 Decorate top with melted chocolate, cool and then cut into squares to serve.

NUTRITIONAL VALUE PER SERVE	FAT 22.5 G	CARBOHYDRATE 42.5 G	PROTEIN 3 G

Apricot brandy slice

INGREDIENTS

90 g dried apricots, chopped
2 tablespoons brandy
100 g dark chocolate
4 tablespoons butter
3 tablespoons milk
1 egg
60 g caster sugar
90 g plain flour, sifted
¼ teaspoon baking powder
chocolate icing
60 g dark chocolate
1 tablespoon milk
250 g icing sugar, sifted
1 tablespoon butter
makes 16

PREPARATION TIME
20 minutes

COOKING TIME
15 minutes

1 Preheat the oven to 180°C. Combine apricots and brandy. Set aside for 15 minutes. Melt chocolate and butter together in a double-boiler and stir in milk, egg, sugar, flour and baking powder. Mix well. Stir apricots through the chocolate mixture.

2 Spoon the mixture into a lightly greased 20 cm square tin. Bake for 12–15 minutes or until firm. Cool in the tin.

3 To make the chocolate icing, melt together the chocolate and milk, and blend in icing sugar and butter. Spread icing evenly over slice.

NUTRITIONAL VALUE PER SERVE   FAT **8.5** G   CARBOHYDRATE **32** G   PROTEIN 2 G

Macadamia caramel squares

INGREDIENTS

base

100 g white chocolate, suitable for melting

125 g butter

90 g icing sugar

60 g macadamia nuts, roasted and ground

200 g plain flour

topping

400 g sweetened condensed milk

200 g milk chocolate, suitable for melting

2 large eggs

2 tablespoons plain flour

90 g shortbread biscuits, chopped, not crushed

200 g macadamia nuts, roasted and roughly chopped

60 g macadamia nuts, roasted

makes 18

1 Preheat the oven to 180°C. To make the base, melt the white chocolate, then add it to a mixer with the butter, icing sugar, macadamia nuts and plain flour.

2 Mix on low speed until all the ingredients are combined, then press the mixture into a greased and lined lamington tin. Bake for 18 minutes, then cool.

3 To make the topping, preheat the oven to 160°C. In a saucepan, heat the condensed milk and milk chocolate together until the chocolate has melted. Add the eggs, flour, shortbread biscuit pieces and chopped macadamia nuts, and mix gently.

4 Pour this mixture over the base, then sprinkle the extra macadamia nuts over. Bake for 40 minutes. Remove from the oven and cool completely in the refrigerator before slicing.

PREPARATION TIME
15 minutes, plus refrigeration time

COOKING TIME
60 minutes

NUTRITIONAL VALUE PER SERVE   FAT 29 G   CARBOHYDRATE 39 G   PROTEIN 7 G

Two-fruit crumble slice

INGREDIENTS

base

125 g butter
125 g brown sugar
100 g milk chocolate, suitable for
  melting
75 g desiccated coconut
125 g sweet biscuits, finely crushed
1 tablespoon cocoa

filling

250 g dried apricots
250 g dried peaches
1 tablespoon honey
juice and zest of 2 oranges
50 ml water

topping

90 g shredded coconut
75 g rolled oats
90 g butter
2 tablespoons golden syrup
60 g cashews, salted, roasted
  and chopped

makes 16

1 Preheat the oven to 180°C. To make the base, place the butter, brown sugar and chocolate in a saucepan and heat gently, stirring well to avoid burning. When the mixture has melted, add the coconut, biscuit and cocoa, and stir vigorously until combined. Press into the base of a greased 20 cm square cake tin and bake for 10 minutes.

2 To make the filling, chop the dried fruit and place in a saucepan with the honey, orange juice, zest and water. Bring to the boil. Reduce heat and simmer for 10 minutes. Allow to cool, then spread over the cooked biscuit base.

3 To make the topping, mix the coconut and oats together, cook in the microwave on high for 2 minutes, then stir gently. Cook for a further minute. In a separate bowl, heat the butter and golden syrup together until bubbling, then stir in the oat mixture and cashews, and mix thoroughly.

4 Sprinkle the topping over the filling, then bake for 15–18 minutes until the topping is golden. Remove from the oven, cool, then slice into 16 even pieces.

PREPARATION TIME
15 minutes

COOKING TIME
40 minutes

NUTRITIONAL VALUE PER SERVE   FAT 23.5 G   CARBOHYDRATE 39 G   PROTEIN 4.5 G

Crunchy gold bars

INGREDIENTS

100 g butter
1/2 cup brown sugar
2 tablespoons golden syrup
2 1/2 cups rolled oats
1/2 cup crushed nuts
1 egg, beaten
extra crushed nuts
makes 48

1 Melt butter, brown sugar and golden syrup in a saucepan over a low heat.

2 Mix oats, nuts, egg and melted butter mixture until well combined.

3 Divide mixture into 4 even portions and shape into bars.

4 Roll each bar in crushed nuts, wrap in foil and set in the refrigerator. Serve cut into small bars.

PREPARATION TIME
15 minutes

| NUTRITIONAL VALUE PER SERVE | FAT 3 G | CARBOHYDRATE 5.5 G | PROTEIN 1 G |

Chocolate-coated muesli fingers

INGREDIENTS

¼ cup honey
3 tablespoons butter
2 eggs
3 cups natural muesli
2 cups chocolate buttons
makes 24

1 Preheat the oven to 180°C.

2 Place the honey and butter into a small saucepan or microwave-safe container. Heat until butter has melted. Cool.

3 Place eggs and muesli into a large mixing bowl, add the honey mixture and stir well to combine. Press mixture into a lightly greased baking tin. Bake for 10 minutes. Cool in tin.

4 Melt the chocolate buttons. Spread chocolate over the top of the cooked muesli mix and allow to set. Cut into fingers.

PREPARATION TIME
30 minutes

COOKING TIME
10 minutes

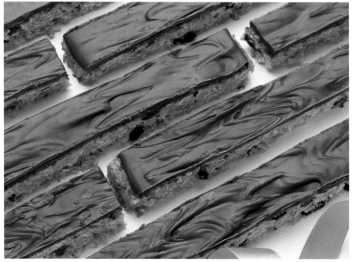

NUTRITIONAL VALUE PER SERVE   FAT **8** G   CARBOHYDRATE **18** G   PROTEIN **2.5** G

Double-fudge blondies

INGREDIENTS

base
250 g butter, softened
375 g sugar
1 teaspoon vanilla extract
4 eggs, lightly beaten
225 g plain flour
¹/₂ teaspoon baking powder
180 g white chocolate, melted
filling
200 g cream cheese, softened
80 g white chocolate, melted
2 tablespoons maple syrup
1 egg
1 tablespoon plain flour
makes 24

PREPARATION TIME
12 minutes

COOKING TIME
45 minutes

1 Preheat the oven to 180°C. To make the filling, place cream cheese, chocolate, maple syrup, egg and flour in a bowl and beat until smooth. Set aside.

2 Place butter, sugar and vanilla extract in a bowl and beat until light and fluffy. Gradually beat in the eggs.

3 Sift together the flour and baking powder over the butter mixture. Add the chocolate and mix well to combine.

4 Spread half the mixture over the base of a greased and lined 23 cm square cake tin. Top with cream cheese filling and then with the remaining mixture. Bake for 45 minutes or until firm. Cool in the tin, then cut into squares.

Note: These lusciously rich white brownies can double as a dessert if drizzled with melted white or dark chocolate and topped with toasted flaked almonds.

NUTRITIONAL VALUE PER SERVE	FAT **16.5** G	CARBOHYDRATE **31** G	PROTEIN **4** G

Chocolate raspberry brownies

INGREDIENTS

1 cup plain flour
2 teaspoons bicarbonate of soda
$^3/_4$ cup cocoa
2 eggs, lightly beaten
1$^1/_4$ cups caster sugar
1 teaspoon vanilla extract
1$^1/_4$ tablespoons sunflower oil
200 g reduced-fat vanilla yoghurt
$^1/_2$ cup apple purée
200 g fresh or frozen raspberries
icing sugar, to dust
fresh berries, to serve
makes 16

PREPARATION TIME
20 minutes

COOKING TIME
30 minutes

1 Preheat the oven to 180°C. Sift the flour, bicarbonate of soda and cocoa into a large bowl and make a well in the centre to prepare for mixing in the wet ingredients.

2 In a large jug, whisk together the eggs, caster sugar, vanilla extract, oil and yoghurt. Add to the flour mixture and mix until smooth. Fold through the apple purée and raspberries.

3 Spoon the mixture into a greased and lined 30 x 20 cm baking tin and bake for 30 minutes or until a skewer comes out clean when inserted in the centre. Allow to cool for 5 minutes in the tin before turning out onto a wire rack to cool completely.

4 Cut into 16 squares and dust with icing sugar. Serve cool or warm with extra fresh berries and cream or ice cream.

NUTRITIONAL VALUE PER SERVE	FAT 3.5 G	CARBOHYDRATE 27 G	PROTEIN 3.5 G

Chocolate and raspberry slice

INGREDIENTS

75 g unsalted butter
75 g plain chocolate, broken into chunks
75 g fresh or frozen raspberries
2 medium eggs, separated
50 g caster sugar
25 g ground almonds
25 g cocoa, sifted
25 g plain flour, sifted
icing sugar, to dust
fresh mint, to garnish
extra raspberries, to garnish
raspberry sauce
150 g fresh or frozen raspberries
1 tablespoon caster sugar (optional)
makes 12

PREPARATION TIME
20 minutes, plus
1 hour cooling

COOKING TIME
25 minutes

1 Preheat the oven to 180°C. Melt the butter and chocolate in a double-boiler, stirring constantly. Cool slightly.

2 Press the raspberries through a sieve. Whisk the egg yolks and sugar until pale and creamy, then mix in the almonds, cocoa, flour, melted chocolate and sieved raspberries.

3 Using an electric whisk, whisk the egg whites until they form stiff peaks. Fold a little into the chocolate mixture to loosen, then fold in the remainder. Spoon into a greased and lined 18 cm loose-bottomed baking tin and cook for 25 minutes or until risen and just firm. Cool for 1 hour.

4 To make the raspberry sauce, sieve the raspberries. Stir in the caster sugar, if using.

5 Remove the cake from the tin and dust with the icing sugar. Serve with the sauce, and decorate with mint and raspberries.

NUTRITIONAL VALUE PER SERVE   FAT 14.5 G   CARBOHYDRATE 18.5 G   PROTEIN 4 G

Chocolate cheesecake slice

INGREDIENTS

base
200 g low-fat digestive biscuits
100 g unsalted butter, at room
   temperature
1 tablespoon white sugar
¼ teaspoon ground cinnamon
   (optional)
filling
400 g cream cheese, at room
   temperature
2 eggs
145 g caster sugar
200 g bittersweet chocolate, broken
   into pieces
145 ml sour cream
1 tablespoon dark rum
115 g strawberries, halved, to decorate
serves 8

1 To make the base, place the biscuits into a plastic bag, then crush with a rolling pin to make crumbs. Place in a large bowl and mix in the butter and sugar. Add the cinnamon, if using, and mix again. Press the mixture evenly into the base and up the sides of a 23 cm flan tin. Refrigerate until needed.

2 Preheat the oven to 180°C. In a large bowl, beat the cheese with a wooden spoon until soft. Lightly beat the eggs in a small bowl, then gradually beat them into the cheese, with the caster sugar. Stir until the mixture is smooth.

3 Melt the chocolate in a double-boiler, stirring frequently. Remove from the heat and stir in the sour cream and the rum.

4 Stir the chocolate mixture into the cheese mixture, then pour over the prepared base. Bake for 30 minutes or until the edges of the mixture look set. Turn the heat off and leave to cool for 1 hour in the oven, with the door open.

5 Place in the fridge for 2 hours before serving.

PREPARATION TIME
15 minutes, plus
1 hour cooling and
2 hours refrigeration

COOKING TIME
30 minutes

NUTRITIONAL VALUE PER SERVE	FAT 46 G	CARBOHYDRATE 53.5 G	PROTEIN 8 G

Lamingtons

INGREDIENTS

sponge

³/₄ cup cornflour

1 teaspoon cream of tartar

¹/₂ teaspoon bicarbonate of soda

¹/₄ cup custard powder

4 eggs, separated and at room temperature

³/₄ cup caster sugar

coating

500 g icing sugar

3 tablespoons cocoa

6–8 tablespoons warm water

50 g desiccated coconut

makes 12

1 To make the sponge, preheat the oven to 200°C. Sift all dry ingredients together (except caster sugar) 3 times. Beat the egg whites until stiff peaks form.

2 Slowly add the caster sugar to the egg whites and continue to beat. Add egg yolks and fold into mixture. Sift in dry ingredients and fold in with a metal spoon. Pour mixture into a greased and lined lamington tin, and bake for approximately 20 minutes. Cool and turn out sponge. Cut the sponge and set aside.

3 To make the coating, sift the icing sugar and cocoa powder into a large bowl. Stir in the water until you have a runny icing. Pour icing into a tray, and place coconut in another tray.

4 Dip cake squares in chocolate icing. Allow excess icing to drain off, then roll in coconut. Place on a wire rack to set.

PREPARATION TIME
25 minutes

COOKING TIME
20 minutes

NUTRITIONAL VALUE PER SERVE	FAT 6 G	CARBOHYDRATE 79.5 G	PROTEIN 6 G

Layered chocolate fingers

INGREDIENTS

150 g butter
2 cups icing sugar, sifted
2 tablespoons cocoa
1 egg
1 teaspoon vanilla extract
250 g milk coffee biscuits
2 tablespoons milk
makes 21

1 Melt butter in a saucepan over a low heat, or in a microwave oven.

2 Mix icing sugar, cocoa, egg, vanilla extract and melted butter until well combined. Cool slightly.

3 Starting and finishing with the chocolate mixture, arrange alternate layers of mixture and milk coffee biscuits in a foil-lined tin, drizzling each layer of biscuit with a little milk. Set in the refrigerator.

PREPARATION TIME
30 minutes, plus refrigeration time

NUTRITIONAL VALUE PER SERVE   FAT **8** G   CARBOHYDRATE **22** G   PROTEIN **1.5** G

Hot brownies with white chocolate sauce

INGREDIENTS

100 g butter, softened
100 g soft dark brown sugar
1 large egg, beaten
1 tablespoon golden syrup
1 tablespoon cocoa, sifted
50 g wholemeal self-raising flour, sifted
25 g pecans or walnuts, chopped
white chocolate sauce
1 tablespoon cornflour
200 ml milk
50 g white chocolate, broken into small chunks
makes 8

1 To make the brownies, preheat the oven to 180°C. Beat the butter and sugar in a bowl until pale and creamy, then beat in the egg, syrup, cocoa and flour until it forms a thick, smooth batter. Stir in the nuts.

2 Spoon the mixture into a greased 18 cm cake tin, smooth the top and bake for 35–40 minutes, until well risen and just firm to the touch.

3 Meanwhile, make the chocolate sauce. Blend the cornflour with 1 tablespoon of the milk. Heat the rest of the milk in a saucepan, add the cornflour mixture, then gently bring to the boil, stirring as the sauce thickens. Cook gently for 1–2 minutes.

4 Add the white chocolate, then remove from the heat and stir until it melts. Cut the brownies into 8 pieces and serve warm with the chocolate sauce.

PREPARATION TIME
15 minutes

COOKING TIME
40 minutes

NUTRITIONAL VALUE PER SERVE   FAT 8 G   CARBOHYDRATE 12.5 G   PROTEIN 1.5 G

Melted chocolate pecan brownies

INGREDIENTS

200 g dark cooking chocolate
100 g butter
1½ cups white sugar
4 eggs
1 cup plain flour
½ teaspoon baking powder
1 teaspoon vanilla extract
½ cup chopped pecans
makes 10–12

PREPARATION TIME
20 minutes

COOKING TIME
35 minutes

1 Preheat the oven to 190°C. Melt the chocolate and butter together in a saucepan over a medium heat.

2 Remove from heat, stir in sugar and cool slightly. Add the eggs and beat with a wooden spoon to combine. Mix in flour, baking powder and vanilla extract until smooth. Mix in pecan nuts.

3 Pour into a greased and lined 20 cm square cake tin.

4 Bake for 30–35 minutes or until brownie mixture is set. Cut into squares.

NUTRITIONAL VALUE PER SERVE   FAT **19** G   CARBOHYDRATE **48.5** G   PROTEIN **5** G

Almond shortbreads

INGREDIENTS

1³/₄ cups clarified butter
¹/₄ cup caster sugar
1 tablespoon vanilla extract
1 cup ground blanched almonds,
  roasted
1 egg yolk
5 cups plain flour
20 cloves
icing sugar, to dust
makes 20

PREPARATION TIME
15 minutes, plus 15
minutes refrigeration

COOKING TIME
15 minutes

1 Preheat the oven to 170°C. Beat the butter with the caster sugar
   until pale and creamy, then add the vanilla extract and almonds
   and mix thoroughly. Add the egg yolk and mix until well combined.
   Sift the flour and fold it into the mixture with a metal spoon until
   well combined.

2 Bring the dough together with your hands and knead lightly
   for 2 minutes until smooth. Wrap in plastic and refrigerate for
   15 minutes.

3 Flatten the dough with your hands to 1–2 cm thick and roll into
   half-moon shapes. Place a clove in the centre of each shortbread,
   place on a greased baking tray and bake for 15 minutes or until
   golden.

4 Remove from the oven, place on a sheet of greaseproof paper and
   (while still hot) sift the icing sugar over the shortbreads until well
   covered. Leave to cool.

NUTRITIONAL VALUE PER SERVE   FAT 22.5 G   CARBOHYDRATE 28 G   PROTEIN 5 G

Orange-pistachio biscotti

INGREDIENTS

2 cups self raising flour
1 cup sugar
pinch salt
2 eggs
2 egg whites
1 tablespoon orange zest, finely
  grated
½ teaspoon vanilla extract
½ cup pistachios, shelled
makes 48

1 Preheat the oven to 180°C. Sift the flour, sugar and salt into a bowl.

2 Place the eggs, egg whites, orange zest and vanilla extract in a separate bowl and whisk to combine.

3 Stir the egg mixture and nuts into the flour mixture and mix to make a smooth dough. Turn the dough onto a floured surface and divide into 2 portions.

4 Roll each portion into a 5 cm thick log. Flatten the logs slightly and place 10 cm apart on a baking tray. Bake for 30 minutes. Remove and set aside to cool. Reduce the oven temperature to 150°C.

5 Cut the cooled logs into 1 cm thick slices, place the cut sides down onto a greased and lined baking tray and bake for 10 minutes or until biscuits are crisp.

6 Biscotti need to be dried out well. Place them in an oven at 75°C for 4 hours. Turn over after 2 hours. Cool on the trays.

PREPARATION TIME
15 minutes

COOKING TIME
30 minutes, plus
4 hours 10 minutes
to crisp

NUTRITIONAL VALUE PER SERVE   FAT 1 G   CARBOHYDRATE 8.5 G   PROTEIN 1 G

Prune and orange biscuits

INGREDIENTS

¹/₂ cup butter
¹/₂ cup icing sugar
zest of 1 orange, grated
¹/₂ cup plain flour
³/₄ cup prunes, pitted and chopped
dark chocolate, suitable for melting
makes 25

PREPARATION TIME
10 minutes

COOKING TIME
15 minutes

1 Preheat the oven to 180°C. Cream together the butter, sugar and orange zest and blend in the flour. Stir the prunes through the mixture.

2 Roll the mixture into small balls and place on a lightly greased oven tray. Flatten with a fork. Bake for 12–15 minutes.

3 Cool for 5 minutes before removing biscuits to a wire rack to cool completely.

4 Decorate the biscuits with melted chocolate.

NUTRITIONAL VALUE PER SERVE	FAT 28 G	CARBOHYDRATE 52G	PROTEIN 3.5 G

Cinnamon and almond crisps

INGREDIENTS

$^1/_2$ cup butter
1 cup caster sugar
1 egg
$^1/_2$ cup plain flour
$^1/_2$ cup almond meal
$^1/_4$ cup self-raising flour
$^3/_4$ teaspoon bicarbonate of soda
2 teaspoons ground cinnamon
makes 25

1 Preheat the oven to 180°C. Place the butter and $^3/_4$ cup of the caster sugar in a bowl and beat until light and fluffy. Add the egg and beat well.

2 Sift together the flour, almond meal, self-raising flour and bicarbonate of soda and stir into the butter mixture.

3 Turn dough onto a floured work surface and knead briefly. Wrap in plastic wrap and refrigerate for 30 minutes or until firm.

4 Place the cinnamon and remaining sugar in a small bowl and mix together. Roll the dough into small balls, then roll the balls in the sugar mixture. Place them 5 cm apart on lightly greased baking trays. Flatten with the back of a spoon and bake for 8 minutes or until golden. Remove to wire racks to cool.

PREPARATION TIME
10 minutes, plus 30 minutes refrigeration

COOKING TIME
8 minutes

NUTRITIONAL VALUE PER SERVE	FAT 5.5 G	CARBOHYDRATE 11.5 G	PROTEIN 1 G

Pecan anzacs

INGREDIENTS

$^1/_2$ cup butter
1 tablespoon golden syrup
1 teaspoon bicarbonate of soda
2 tablespoons boiling water
1 cup rolled oats
$^3/_4$ cup desiccated coconut
$^1/_2$ cup plain flour
1 cup sugar
$^1/_2$ cup pecans, chopped
makes 48

1 Preheat the oven to 180°C. Melt the butter and golden syrup in a saucepan. Dissolve the bicarbonate of soda in the boiling water and add to the syrup.

2 Combine the oats, coconut, flour, sugar and pecans. Pour the melted mixture over the dry ingredients and mix well. Place teaspoonfuls of the mixture onto greased oven trays, allowing room for spreading.

3 Bake for 15 minutes or until golden. Cool the biscuits for a few minutes on the tray before removing to a wire rack to cool completely.

PREPARATION TIME
10 minutes

COOKING TIME
15 minutes

NUTRITIONAL VALUE PER SERVE	FAT 4 G	CARBOHYDRATE 7 G	PROTEIN 0.5 G

Almond cakes

INGREDIENTS

3½ cups blanched almonds
1 cup caster sugar
2 medium eggs
½ cup soft white breadcrumbs
⅓ cup honey, warmed to liquid
makes 38–40

PREPARATION TIME
10 minutes

COOKING TIME
15 minutes

1 Preheat the oven to 180°C. Grind the almonds in a food processor with a little of the sugar. Combine the remaining sugar with the eggs, and whisk until pale, thick and creamy. Add the ground almonds and the breadcrumbs, and stir until well combined.

2 Using a tablespoon, shape mixture roughly into diamond shapes and place on a greased baking tray. Bake for 15 minutes.

3 While warm, place the cakes on wire cooling racks and brush with the honey. Allow to cool a little before serving.

NUTRITIONAL VALUE PER SERVE   FAT **8** G   CARBOHYDRATE **9** G   PROTEIN **3** G

Date and orange biscuits

INGREDIENTS

¹/₂ cup light soft brown sugar
¹/₂ cup caster sugar
³/₄ cup butter
zest of 1 orange, finely grated
1 medium egg
1 cup self-raising wholemeal flour
1 cup rolled oats
¹/₂ cup dried dates, finely chopped
makes 45

PREPARATION TIME
12 minutes

COOKING TIME
15 minutes

1 Preheat the oven to 180°C. Place the sugars and the butter in a bowl and beat together until light and fluffy. Add the orange zest, then gradually beat in the egg. Fold in the flour and oats, then fold in the dates and combine.

2 Place heaped teaspoonfuls of the mixture onto greased baking trays, spacing well apart to allow the biscuits to spread during baking. Bake for 15 minutes or until golden brown.

3 Cool slightly on the baking trays, then transfer to a wire rack to cool completely.

NUTRITIONAL VALUE PER SERVE   FAT 4.5 G   CARBOHYDRATE 13 G   PROTEIN 1.5 G

Blueberry chocolate soft-bake biscuits

INGREDIENTS

145 g plain flour
1½ teaspoons baking powder
1 teaspoon ground cinnamon
55 g butter, cubed
85 g brown sugar
100 ml milk
100 g fresh blueberries
55 g white chocolate chips
makes 8 large biscuits

PREPARATION TIME
10 minutes

COOKING TIME
20 minutes

1 Preheat the oven to 190°C. Liberally grease a baking tray with butter.

2 Sift the flour, baking powder and cinnamon into a bowl. Rub in the butter, until the mixture resembles rough breadcrumbs, then stir in the sugar.

3 Stir in the milk, blueberries and chocolate chips until just combined (the dough will be quite sticky). Spoon 8 mounds, spaced well apart, onto a tray and bake for 20 minutes or until golden and springy to the touch. Cool on a wire rack for a few minutes before serving.

NUTRITIONAL VALUE PER SERVE   FAT **8.5** G   CARBOHYDRATE **29** G   PROTEIN **3** G

Coconut chocolate creams

INGREDIENTS

125 g butter
³/₄ cup brown sugar
1 teaspoon vanilla extract
2 eggs
1 cup coconut
1¹/₂ cups plain flour
2 tablespoons cocoa
1 teaspoon baking powder
filling
2 tablespoons butter
1¹/₂ cups pure icing sugar
1 tablespoon cocoa
3 tablespoons coconut cream powder
1–2 tablespoons water
makes 12 pairs

1 Preheat the oven to 180°C. Melt the butter in a saucepan large enough to mix all the ingredients. Remove from the heat and mix in sugar and vanilla extract.

2 Add eggs and beat with a wooden spoon until combined. Add coconut and sift in flour, cocoa and baking powder. Mix until combined.

3 Roll teaspoons of mixture into balls. Place on a greased oven tray, allowing room to spread. Flatten with a fork.

4 Bake for 12–15 minutes or until cooked. Cool on a wire rack.

5 To make the filling, melt butter. Place icing sugar, cocoa and coconut cream powder in a bowl, mixing together. Mix in butter and enough water to make a spreadable filling. Sandwich biscuits together with filling.

PREPARATION TIME
20 minutes

COOKING TIME
15 minutes

NUTRITIONAL VALUE PER SERVE   FAT **17.5** G   CARBOHYDRATE **40.5** G   PROTEIN **4** G

Chocolate dot cookies

INGREDIENTS

$^1/_2$ cup caster sugar
$^1/_2$ cup brown sugar
175 g butter
$^1/_2$ teaspoon vanilla extract
1 egg
$^3/_4$ plain flour
1 cup self-raising flour
1$^1/_2$ cups chocolate buttons, suitable
   for cooking
makes 36

1 Preheat the oven to 180°C. Place sugars and butter into a medium-sized mixing bowl. Using an electric beater, mix until creamy.

2 Add vanilla extract and egg and mix again until well combined.

3 Sift together the plain and self-raising flour. Add to the creamed butter and sugar and mix in well using a wooden spoon. Stir in the chocolate buttons.

4 Place teaspoonfuls of mixture onto lightly greased oven trays.

5 Bake for 15 minutes. Cool on tray for 5 minutes before removing to a wire tray to cool.

PREPARATION TIME
5 minutes

COOKING TIME
15 minutes

NUTRITIONAL VALUE PER SERVE	FAT 6.5 G	CARBOHYDRATE 14 G	PROTEIN 1.5 G

Choc-almond biscotti

INGREDIENTS

2 cups plain flour
$1/2$ cup cocoa
1 teaspoon bicarbonate of soda
$1/4$ cup butter, melted
2 tablespoons milk
2 tablespoons dark rum
1 cup sugar
200 g blanched almonds
2 eggs
1 egg yolk
makes 35

1 Preheat the oven to 180°C. Sift together the flour, cocoa and bicarbonate of soda into a bowl. Mix in the butter, milk and rum. Make a well in the centre of the mixture, add the sugar, almonds and eggs and mix well to form a soft dough.

2 Turn the dough onto a lightly floured work surface and knead until smooth. Divide the dough into four equal portions. Roll out each portion of dough to make a strip 5 mm thick and 4 cm wide.

3 Place the strips on a greased and lined baking tray. Brush with the egg yolk and bake for 30 minutes or until lightly browned. Cut the strips into 1 cm slices, return to the baking tray, and bake for 10 minutes longer or until dry.

PREPARATION TIME
15 minutes

COOKING TIME
40 minutes

NUTRITIONAL VALUE PER SERVE   FAT 5.5 G   CARBOHYDRATE 12.5 G   PROTEIN 2.5 G

Double chocolate chip biscuits

INGREDIENTS

200 g butter
3 tablespoons cocoa
2 teaspoons vanilla extract
$\frac{1}{2}$ cup icing sugar
$1\frac{1}{4}$ cups plain flour
$\frac{1}{4}$ cup cornflour
1 cup chocolate chips, suitable for
   cooking
makes 18

PREPARATION TIME
20 minutes

COOKING TIME
20 minutes

1 Preheat the oven to 180°C. Melt the butter with the cocoa in a saucepan large enough to mix all the ingredients. Remove from heat and add vanilla extract.

2 Sift together the icing sugar, flour and cornflour. Mix with cocoa mixture until partly combined, then add chocolate chips and mix until thoroughly combined.

3 Take about two tablespoons of mixture at a time, roll into balls and place on a greased oven tray. Flatten with the back of a spoon.

4 Bake for 15–20 minutes or until biscuits are just starting to colour. Cool on the tray until firm, then remove to a wire rack.

Note: Macadamia nuts are often used in combination with chocolate chips. Try them in these biscuits or add chopped walnuts or pecans. If you want to make a biscuit without the chocolate chips but with other goodies, use this as a basic recipe, omitting the chocolate chips and substituting the ingredients of your choice.

NUTRITIONAL VALUE PER SERVE	FAT **12.5** G	CARBOHYDRATE **18** G	PROTEIN **2** G

Night-sky biscuits

INGREDIENTS

¹/₂ cup butter, softened
1 cup caster sugar
¹/₂ teaspoon almond essence
1 egg, lightly beaten
2 cups plain flour
¹/₂ teaspoon baking powder
¹/₄ cup milk
¹/₂ cup white chocolate, melted
1 cup dark chocolate, melted
makes 24

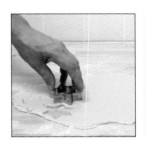

PREPARATION TIME
20 minutes

COOKING TIME
10 minutes

1 Preheat the oven to 180°C. Place the butter, caster sugar and almond essence in a bowl and beat until light and fluffy. Gradually beat in the egg.

2 Sift together the flour and baking powder. Fold the flour mixture and the milk, alternately, into the butter mixture and mix to form a soft dough.

3 Roll out the dough onto a lightly floured work surface to 5 mm thick. Using a star- and a moon-shaped cutter, cut out the biscuits. Place them on lightly greased baking trays and bake for 10 minutes or until biscuits are golden and cooked. Transfer to wire racks to cool.

4 Dip the tops of the moon-shaped biscuits in the white chocolate and the tips of the star-shaped biscuits in the dark chocolate. Place on wire racks to set.

NUTRITIONAL VALUE PER SERVE	FAT 6 G	CARBOHYDRATE 20 G	PROTEIN 2 G

Choc layer biscuits

INGREDIENTS

115 g butter
1 cup brown sugar
$^3/_4$ cup sugar
2 teaspoons vanilla extract
1 egg
2$^3/_4$ cups plain flour
1 teaspoon baking powder
$^1/_2$ cup cocoa
$^1/_2$ cup malted milk powder
makes 40

PREPARATION TIME
16 minutes, plus
1 hour chilling

COOKING TIME
15 minutes

1 Preheat the oven to 180°C. Place the butter, brown sugar, sugar and vanilla extract in a bowl and beat until light and fluffy.

2 Add the egg and beat well. Sift together the flour and the baking powder. Add the flour mixture to the butter mixture to form a soft dough.

3 Divide the dough into two equal portions. Knead the cocoa into one portion and the malted milk powder into the other.

4 Roll out each portion of dough on greaseproof paper to make a 20 x 30 cm rectangle. Place the chocolate dough on top of the malt dough and press together. Cut in half lengthwise and place one half of dough on top of the other. You should now have 4 layers of dough in alternating colours. Place the layered dough on a tray, cover with plastic wrap and refrigerate for 1 hour.

5 Cut the dough into 1 cm wide fingers and place on greased baking trays. Bake for 15 minutes. Transfer to wire racks to cool.

NUTRITIONAL VALUE PER SERVE	FAT 3 G	CARBOHYDRATE 15.5 G	PROTEIN 2 G

Almond and white chocolate macaroons

INGREDIENTS

200 g marzipan
1 cup caster sugar
2 large egg whites
½ cup toasted, flaked almonds
filling
¼ cup cream
45 g unsalted butter
zest of 1 orange, grated
170 g white chocolate, suitable for
  cooking, chopped
serves 10

PREPARATION TIME
30 minutes

COOKING TIME
10 minutes

1 Preheat the oven to 175°C. Process the marzipan, caster sugar and egg whites in a food processor until thoroughly combined.

2 Spoon the mixture onto two greased baking trays, making it into finger-size lengths. Leave space around each macaroon. Place almonds on each biscuit and bake for 10 minutes. Cool on the trays for 5 minutes, then transfer the biscuits to a wire rack to cool completely.

3 To make the filling, bring the cream, butter and orange zest to a simmer in a small saucepan, then add the chocolate and stir until smooth. Remove from the heat, and let the filling cool until thick: about 15 minutes.

4 When the biscuits are completely cold, sandwich them together with filling.

NUTRITIONAL VALUE PER SERVE   FAT **18** G   CARBOHYDRATE **43** G   PROTEIN **4.5** G

Glossary

Al dente: Italian term to describe pasta and rice that are cooked until tender but still firm to the bite.

Asafoetida: a herbaceous perennial plant native to Iran. The dried sap is used as a spice. It resembles onion and garlic in flavour.

Bake blind: to bake pastry cases without their fillings. Line the raw pastry case with greaseproof paper and fill with raw rice or dried beans to prevent collapsed sides and puffed base. Remove paper and fill 5 minutes before completion of cooking time.

Baste: to spoon hot cooking liquid over food at intervals during cooking to moisten and flavour it.

Beat: to make a mixture smooth with rapid and regular motions using a spatula, wire whisk or electric mixer; to make a mixture light and smooth by enclosing air.

Beurre manié: equal quantities of butter and flour mixed together to a smooth paste and stirred bit by bit into a soup, stew or sauce while on the heat to thicken. Stop adding when desired thickness results.

Bind: to add egg or a thick sauce to hold ingredients together when cooked.

Blanch: to plunge some foods into boiling water for less than a minute and immediately plunge into iced water. This is to brighten the colour of some vegetables; to remove skin from tomatoes and nuts.

Blend: to mix 2 or more ingredients thoroughly together; do not confuse with blending in an electric blender.

Boil: to cook in a liquid brought to boiling point and kept there.

Boiling point: when bubbles rise continually and break over the entire surface of the liquid, reaching a temperature of 100°C (212°F). In some cases food is held at this high temperature for a few seconds then heat is turned to low for slower cooking. See simmer.

Bouquet garni: a bundle of several herbs tied together with string for easy removal, placed into pots of stock, soups and stews for flavour. A few sprigs of fresh thyme, parsley and bay leaf are used. Can be purchased in sachet form for convenience.

Caramelise: to heat sugar in a heavy-based pan until it liquefies and develops a caramel colour. Vegetables such as blanched carrots and sautéed onions may be sprinkled with sugar and caramelised.

Chill: to place in the refrigerator or stir over ice until cold.

Clarify: to make a liquid clear by removing sediments and impurities. To melt fat and remove any sediment.

Coat: to dust or roll food items in flour to cover the surface before the food is cooked. Also, to coat in flour, egg and breadcrumbs.

Cool: to stand at room temperature until some or all heat is removed, e.g. cool a little, cool completely.

Cream: to make creamy and fluffy by working the mixture with the back of a wooden spoon, usually refers to creaming butter and sugar or margarine. May also be creamed with an electric mixer.

Croutons: small cubes of bread, toasted or fried, used as an addition to salads or as a garnish to soups and stews.

Crudite: raw vegetable sticks served with a dipping sauce.

Crumb: to coat foods in flour, egg and breadcrumbs to form a protective coating for foods which are fried. Also adds flavour, texture and enhances appearance.

Cube: to cut into small pieces with six even sides, e.g. cubes of meat.

Cut in: to combine fat and flour using 2 knives scissor fashion or with a pastry blender, to make pastry.

Deglaze: to dissolve dried out cooking juices left on the base and sides of a roasting dish or frying pan. Add a little water, wine or stock, scrape and stir over heat until dissolved. Resulting liquid is used to make a flavoursome gravy or added to a sauce or casserole.

Degrease: to skim fat from the surface of cooking liquids, e.g. stocks, soups, casseroles.

Dice: to cut into small cubes.

Dredge: to heavily coat with icing sugar, sugar, flour or cornflour.

Dressing: a mixture added to completed dishes to add moisture and flavour, e.g. salads, cooked vegetables.

Drizzle: to pour in a fine thread-like stream moving over a surface.

Egg wash: beaten egg with milk or water used to brush over pastry, bread dough or biscuits to give a sheen and golden brown colour.

Essence: a strong flavouring liquid, usually made by distillation. Only a few drops are needed to flavour.

Fillet: a piece of prime meat, fish or poultry which is boneless or has all bones removed.

Flake: to separate cooked fish into flakes, removing any bones and skin, using 2 forks.

Flame: to ignite warmed alcohol over food or to pour into a pan with food, ignite then serve.

Flute: to make decorative indentations around the pastry rim before baking.

Fold in: combining of a light, whisked or creamed mixture with other ingredients. Add a portion of the other ingredients at a time and mix using a gentle circular motion, over and under the mixture so that air will not be lost. Use a silver spoon or spatula.

Glaze: to brush or coat food with a liquid that will give the finished product a glossy appearance, and on baked products, a golden brown colour.

Grease: to rub the surface of a metal or heatproof dish with oil or fat, to prevent the food from sticking.

Herbed butter: softened butter mixed with finely chopped fresh herbs and re-chilled. Used to serve on grilled meats and fish.

Hors d'oeuvre: small savoury foods served as an appetiser, popularly known today as 'finger food'.

Infuse: to steep foods in a liquid until the liquid absorbs their flavour.

Joint: to cut poultry and game into serving pieces by dividing at the joint.

Julienne: to cut some food, e.g. vegetables and processed meats, into fine strips the length of matchsticks. Used for inclusion in salads or as a garnish to cooked dishes.

Knead: to work a yeast dough in a pressing, stretching and folding motion with the heel of the hand until smooth and elastic to develop the gluten strands. Non-yeast doughs should be lightly and quickly handled as gluten development is not desired.

Line: to cover the inside of a baking tin with paper for the easy removal of the cooked product from the baking tin.

Macerate: to stand fruit in a syrup, liqueur or spirit to give added flavour.

Marinade: a flavoured liquid, into which food is placed for some time to give it flavour and to tenderise. Marinades include an acid ingredient such as vinegar or wine, oil and seasonings.

Mask: to evenly cover cooked food portions with a sauce, mayonnaise or savoury jelly.

Pan-fry: to fry foods in a small amount of fat or oil, sufficient to coat the base of the pan.

Parboil: to boil until partially cooked. The food is then finished by some other method.

Pare: to peel the skin from vegetables and fruit. Peel is the popular term but pare is the name given to the knife used; paring knife.

Pit: to remove stones or seeds from olives, cherries, dates.

Pith: the white lining between the rind and flesh of oranges, grapefruit and lemons.

Pitted: the olives, cherries, dates etc. with the stone removed, e.g. purchase pitted dates.

Poach: to simmer gently in enough hot liquid to almost cover the food so shape will be retained.

Pound: to flatten meats with a meat mallet; to reduce to a paste or small particles with a mortar and pestle.

Simmer: to cook in liquid just below boiling point at about 96°C (205°F) with small bubbles rising gently to the surface.

Skim: to remove fat or froth from the surface of simmering food.

Stock: the liquid produced when meat, poultry, fish or vegetables have been simmered in water to extract the flavour. Used as a base for soups, sauces, casseroles etc. Convenience stock products are available.

Sweat: to cook sliced onions or vegetables, in a small amount of butter in a covered pan over low heat, to soften them and release flavour without colouring.

Conversions

Measurements differ from country to country, so it's important to understand what the differences are. This Measurements Guide gives you simple 'at-a-glance' information for using the recipes in this book, wherever you may be.

Cooking is not an exact science – minor variations in measurements won't make a difference to your cooking.

EQUIPMENT

There is a difference in the size of measuring cups used internationally, but the difference is minimal (only 2–3 teaspoons). We use the Australian standard metric measurements in our recipes:

1 teaspoon ....5 ml	1 tablespoon....20 ml
^{1}/2 cup......125 ml	1 cup.....250 ml
4 cups...1 litre	

Measuring cups come in sets of one cup (250 ml), 1/2 cup (125 ml), 1/3 cup (80 ml) and 1/4 cup (60 ml). Use these for measuring liquids and certain dry ingredients.

Measuring spoons come in a set of four and should be used for measuring dry and liquid ingredients.

When using cup or spoon measures always make them level (unless the recipe indicates otherwise).

DRY VERSUS WET INGREDIENTS

While this system of measures is consistent for liquids, it's more difficult to quantify dry ingredients. For instance, one level cup equals: 200 g of brown sugar; 210 g of caster sugar; and 110 g of icing sugar.

When measuring dry ingredients such as flour, don't push the flour down or shake it into the cup. It is best just to spoon the flour in until it reaches the desired amount. When measuring liquids use a clear vessel indicating metric levels.

Always use medium eggs (55–60 g) when eggs are required in a recipe.

OVEN

Your oven should always be at the right temperature before placing the food in it to be cooked. Note that if your oven doesn't have a fan you may need to cook food for a little longer.

MICROWAVE

It is difficult to give an exact cooking time for microwave cooking. It is best to watch what you are cooking closely to monitor its progress.

STANDING TIME

Many foods continue to cook when you take them out of the oven or microwave. If a recipe states that the food needs to 'stand' after cooking, be sure not to overcook the dish.

CAN SIZES

The can sizes available in your supermarket or grocery store may not be the same as specified in the recipe. Don't worry if there is a small variation in size – it's unlikely to make a difference to the end result.

dry		liquids	
metric (grams)	imperial (ounces)	metric (millilitres)	imperial (fluid ounces)
		30 ml	1 fl oz
30 g	1 oz	60 ml	2 fl oz
60 g	2 oz	90 ml	3 fl oz
90 g	3 oz	100 ml	3 $\frac{1}{2}$ fl oz
100 g	3 $\frac{1}{2}$ oz	125 ml	4 fl oz
125 g	4 oz	150 ml	5 fl oz
150 g	5 oz	190 ml	6 fl oz
185 g	6 oz	250 ml	8 fl oz
200 g	7 oz	300 ml	10 fl oz
250 g	8 oz	500 ml	16 fl oz
280 g	9 oz	600 ml	20 fl oz (1 pint)*
315 g	10 oz	1000 ml (1 litre)	32 fl oz
330 g	11 oz		
370 g	12 oz		
400 g	13 oz		
440 g	14 oz		
470 g	15 oz		
500 g	16 oz (1 lb)		
750 g	24 oz (1 $\frac{1}{2}$ lb)		
1000 g (1 kg)	32 oz (2 lb)		*Note: an American pint is 16 fl oz.

cooking temperatures	°C (celsius)	°F (fahrenheit)	gas mark
very slow	120	250	$\frac{1}{2}$
slow	150	300	2
moderately slow	160	315	2–3
moderate	180	350	4
moderate hot	190	375	5
	200	400	6
hot	220	425	7
very hot	230	450	8
	240	475	9
	250	500	10

Index

A

almonds
  almond and white chocolate
    macaroons   56–57
  almond cakes   40–41
  almond shortbreads   32–33
  choc-almond biscotti   49
  cinnamon and almond crisps   38
apricots
  apricot brandy slice   10–11
  two-fruit crumble slice   14–15

B

biscotti
  choc-almond biscotti   49
  orange-pistachio biscotti   34–35
brownies
  chocolate raspberry
    brownies   20–21
  hot brownies with white
    chocolate sauce   28–29
  melted chocolate pecan
    brownies   30–31
blondies
  double-fudge blondies   18–19
blueberry chocolate soft-bake
  biscuits   44–45

C

caramel
  macadamia caramel squares 12–13
cheesecake
  chocolate cheesecake slice   24–25
chocolate
  almond and white chocolate
    macaroons   56–57
  apricot brandy slice   10–11
  blueberry chocolate soft-bake
    biscuits   44–45

choc-almond biscotti   49
choc layer biscuits   54–55
chocolate and raspberry
  slice   22–23
chocolate cheesecake slice   24–25
chocolate-coated muesli fingers 17
chocolate dot cookies   48
chocolate raspberry
  brownies   20–21
coconut chocolate creams   46–47
double chocolate chip
  biscuits   50–51
double-fudge blondies   18–19
fruit medley slice   8–9
hot brownies with white
  chocolate sauce   28–29
lamingtons   26
layered chocolate fingers   27
melted chocolate pecan
  brownies   30–31
night-sky biscuits   52–53
cinnamon and almond crisps   38
coconut
  coconut chocolate creams   46–47
  fruit medley slice   8–9
  lamingtons   26
conversions   60–61
crunchy gold bars   16

D

date
  date and orange biscuits   42–43
double chocolate chip biscuits 50–51
double-fudge blondies   18–19

F

fruit
  apricot brandy slice   10–11
  blueberry chocolate soft-bake
    biscuits   44–45

chocolate raspberry
    brownies   20–21
chocolate and raspberry
    slice   22–23
date and orange biscuits   42–43
fruit medley slice   8–9
prune and orange biscuits   36–37
two-fruit crumble slice   14–15

G
glossary   58–59

H
hot brownies with white
    chocolate sauce   28–29

I
introduction   4–7

L
lamingtons   26
layered chocolate fingers   27

M
macadamia caramel squares   12–13
macaroons
    almond and white chocolate
        macaroons   56–57
melted chocolate pecan
    brownies   30–31
muesli
    chocolate-coated muesli
        fingers   17

N
night-sky biscuits   52–53

O
oats
    crunchy gold bars   16
    date and orange biscuits   57

pecan anzacs   39
    two-fruit crumble slice   14–15
orange
    date and orange biscuits   42–43
    orange-pistachio biscotti   34–35
    prune and orange biscuits   36–37

P
peaches
    two-fruit crumble slice   14–15
pecans
    melted chocolate pecan
        brownies   30–31
    pecan anzacs   39
pistachio
    orange-pistachio biscotti   34–35
prune and orange biscuits   36–37

R
raspberry
    chocolate and raspberry
        slice   22–23
    chocolate raspberry
        brownies   20–21

S
shortbreads
    almond shortbread   32–33

T
two-fruit crumble slice   14–15